T0131602

Continuing your Peanut Power journey

Another Taste
of
Peanut Power

Avril Ann Lochhead

Illustrations by David Lochhead

BALBOA.
PRESS

A DIVISION OF HAY HOUSE

Balboa Press books may be ordered through booksellers or by contacting:

Balboa Press
A Division of Hay House
1663 Liberty Drive
Bloomington, IN 47403
www.balboapress.com.au
1 (877) 407-4847

Print information available on the last page.

ISBN: 978-1-5043-1087-1 (sc)
ISBN: 978-1-5043-1088-8 (e)

Balboa Press rev. date: 11/17/2017

Further food for thought

Peanut Power

and

More Peanut Power

When very young, an elephant is tied to a short rope, fastened to a stake in the ground.

This trains the elephant to stay within the limitations of the immediate area.

Even when fully grown, the elephant is not aware that freedom is there for the taking.

We, like the elephant, have been conditioned.

Our habitual attitudes, thoughts and even feelings can immobilise us.

Our thoughts are our most powerful tools and fuel of creation.

We can use them negatively, or as suggested in this offering of peanuts, we can tap into our potential, unlimited greatness.

Add these peanuts to your daily diet, and move in the direction of your dreams.

Allow them to enrich your experience of living, loving, and embrace your magnificence.

Have fun and play with these peanuts of thought.

Follow their trail to freedom!

*A*bundance

is your birthright.

Abundance is a state of mind in which you are relaxed in the awareness that you have enough of everything.

Sufficient money, time, love and energy to feel fulfilled.

To enable abundance to be real you will be conscious of your spending habits, and if necessary change some.

This page is for you to open your peanut

Your thoughts

Your feelings

Next steps

Budget

for more of life.

Whatever thoughts you have racing through your mind - get them out onto paper.
This increases your effectiveness once you see where your money or energy are going.

This step is vital to your financial well-being.

There seems to be a cultural disease called "Not Enough".

Without taking conscious action you are left "wondering" rather that "knowing" you have enough.

When you are consciously aware of your finances, initiating appropriate action when necessary to address any perceived limitations - the disease disappears.

This page is for you to open your peanut

Your thoughts

Your feelings

Next steps

Challenge

is the way to the cure.

Part of our human make-up is not the slightest bit interested in "doing the work" to lessen the concern of having insufficient money, time, love etc.

This part thrives on you staying as sweet as you are, in the dark with limited, if any power.

Once you turn on the light and illuminate your spending habits, you take the control away from the procrastination habit.

You have the choice in every dollar and minute spent.

This page is for you to open your peanut

Your thoughts

Your feelings

Next steps

$\mathcal{D}$ecide

that you are successful - NOW!

Stand tall, express your dignity,
be confident of the future you are creating,
even when it's not yet visible...
you've made it!

Not necessarily by society's standards
- by your own standards.

This is the beginning of the end of any struggle.

It takes courage, trust and a knowledge about
your Self that gives you peace.

This page is for you to open your peanut

Your thoughts

Your feelings

Next steps

E*nough*

is Enough!

Who says? You do, in your life.

When you have enough, are doing enough, are listening internally enough, and are listening externally enough...

You are indeed enough.

Your life is in a state called Self actualisation. Each facet is brilliant in its entirety.

Together, all that makes up "you" accesses a new, heightened awareness.

There will be Self defined freedom regarding what matters and what fulfills you that you express more fully.

This page is for you to open your peanut

Your thoughts

Your feelings

Next steps

*F*eelings

need to be trusted if you are on the pathway to Self reliance.

Listen quietly and closely to the small voice which will, when given the opportunity, transform your negative thoughts, actions and reactions into acceptance and embracing life.

Practice turning down the volume on demeaning and negative judgements and assessments of yourself and also of others.

Turn up the volume on intuition, trust and reliance on your Self until it becomes your natural expression and way of life.

This page is for you to open your peanut

Your thoughts

Your feelings

Next steps

Goals

is still such a buzzword.

Selectively allow other agendas and goals into your life-space.

Sometimes we leave our Selves too depleted to attain our own goals.

Simple sabotage.

You will need clarity, energy, commitment and trust to permit your purpose to unfold and blossom to your full potential.

Say "Yes" to yourSelf more, and "No" to others if necessary.

This page is for you to open your peanut

Your thoughts

Your feelings

Next steps

$\mathcal{H}$abits

are really contrary.

They have assuredly got you where you are right now, but they may not make room for a fuller expression of you.

There is a part of you wanting to be "safe", risk free, surviving - not necessarily satisfied or fulfilled.

Pick a couple of negative habits, ones that do zero to support your physical well-being or financial health.

Replace them with 2 positive habits - providing you with new and productive experiences in those important areas of life.

Keep a picture of this new you everywhere as it will inspire you to stay on track.

It's wonderful to be willing!

This page is for you to open your peanut

Your thoughts

Your feelings

Next steps

Ignorance

they say is bliss.

Not so sure about that.

Seems that misunderstanding and miscommunication flourish in ignorance which is not my kind of Blissful existence.

Being unaware can be reactive as opposed to responsive.

If we actively raise our level of Self-awareness to enable us to unplug from negative reactions -

we can then have a reaction - and not be the reaction.

This page is for you to open your peanut

Your thoughts

Your feelings

Next steps

Judging

ourselves and others negatively is one of the most destructive practices in your relationship with yourself, and obviously takes a toll on your relationship with others.

Judge yourself kindly, and stop judging others.

They will probably be doing a perfectly great job of judging themselves.

There is no joy in judgement.

This page is for you to open your peanut

Your thoughts

Your feelings

Next steps

Kindness

seems to have become a dying art.

We seem to be programmed for consumerism and our energy is spent on getting, rather than gratitude.

Not only spending our money - also our lives.

A simple act in giving from the love of life, no agenda, can have the most extraordinary influence.

They and you may never be the same.

Free to be!

Satisfyingly Self-enhancing.

This page is for you to open your peanut

Your thoughts

Your feelings

Next steps

Love

makes to world go around.

All you need is love.

If you are not conducting the most profound love affair on the planet with yourSelf - you are really missing out.

Keep acknowledging every step forward, always appreciating your courage on this life's path.

Share your journey with others as love is contagious.

This page is for you to open your peanut

Your thoughts

Your feelings

Next steps

Manage

yourself.
Be real
Be ethical
Be expressed
Do not sell out on you, as you are priceless, unique.

A planetary treasure trove.
Keep discovering more beauty and truth about yourself and you'll be so happy.

Then, when you think you cannot possibly be happier
- you will find even more happiness.

It is in you - nowhere else.

This page is for you to open your peanut

Your thoughts

Your feelings

Next steps

$\mathcal{N}$uisance

is ok.
Be a bit of a cultural nuisance.
Know your facts and take a stand for something worthwhile.

Fill your life-space being brilliantly non-conformist.

This may confront you, parts of you will be saying "Wrong way - go back!"

By being aware and trusting your Self you will be able turn down the noise.

. Be Brave - stand up and be counted - use your voice to make your difference.

This page is for you to open your peanut

Your thoughts

Your feelings

Next steps

*O*penness

does not necessarily
come naturally.

Be honesty in action, true to your
evolving Self.
Tell one on yourself.

When I was in my 20's I lied on an Insurance
claim and received $800.

Years later, whilst participating in an
extraordinary leadership training, the
foundation of which was Integrity, it was time
to immediately come clean.

I called the Insurance Company and asked to
speak to their "Fraudulent Claims Department.
They didn't have one!

I explained I had made a fraudulently claim,
apologised profusely, and immediately sent my
cheque for $800 and watched in anticipation as
the funds were deducted.

I felt completely energised and free.

This page is for you to open your peanut

Your thoughts

Your feelings

Next steps

Peace

within your Self is paramount.

Through non-resistance you can establish a healthy detachment to your life looking a certain way.

Challenge your Status Quo.

Delete a few Self-defeating habits.
Move away from disempowering circumstances.

Allow peace to be your way.

This page is for you to open your peanut

Your thoughts

Your feelings

Next steps

Quiet

reflection is a powerful tool and foundation for growth.

In the quiet, questions are answered and clarity gained.

Think deeply, contribute your gems powerfully, and go about your business of living a life of loving revolution.

Every interaction, each moment matters, we only ever have now!

Have a voice, be heard in matters that are of importance to you.

This page is for you to open your peanut

Your thoughts

Your feelings

Next steps

Reasonableness

might be an aspect of living that could be challenged.

Many life lessons are highly unreasonable. Only you can say if you are selling out.

Being reasonable could be the "lid" on your personal growth and development.

Take risks, be audacious, respect yourself and others.

Create a fabulous future - now - that may be very unreasonable!

This page is for you to open your peanut

Your thoughts

Your feelings

Next steps

Surrender

fully to your Self-expression.

Be a bearer of light and love.
Bigger, wider, more expansive than you
ever imagined.

Be a fountain of fabulousness and fun!

Satisfied, competent, alive and alert to
the wonders of each day.

This page is for you to open your peanut

Your thoughts

Your feelings

Next steps

$\mathcal{T}_{rust}$

that you are on track - even when you seem off-track.
You are exactly where you are meant to be.

Learn about yourself and your journey.
Use this understanding to enhance your experience.

It is easy to be successful when you are on track.
Can you feel equally as successful when you feel off-track?

Trusting, and believing in the invisible, leads to resilience and growth.

This page is for you to open your peanut

Your thoughts

Your feelings

Next steps

Understanding

that everything that has happened was meant to happen, may not be good news.

What if we selected this life's lessons before we even arrived?

All our past – previously planned for our growth and development.

Embrace the reality of your life, let the past be past, step through any fear into a deeper experience of peace and love.

Perfect in your imperfection.

We are all "Works of ART" in progress.

This page is for you to open your peanut

Your thoughts

Your feelings

Next steps

$\mathcal{V}$ision

plus action, makes all the difference.

Having a clear vision for your family, your community, organisations which inspire you all receiving the most fabulous and profound contribution you are capable of making.

This is the stuff of greatness right now!

"Go for something worth failing for!"

This page is for you to open your peanut

Your thoughts

Your feelings

Next steps

Willingness

is one of the keys.

Be willing to let go.
Old ideas, old clothes, old furniture, etc.

You are not your past - Your potential is unlimited - please refrain from labelling yourself or anyone else.

All that is assured is change, so go with the flow of your evolution, enjoy the ride, relish it.

You might as well - This IS your life!

This page is for you to open your peanut

Your thoughts

Your feelings

Next steps

Xplaining

takes a lot of energy.
Like "What happened
to the "e"?" *LOL!*

Sometimes more time and energy than it's worth.

Some people will understand you, some will not.

Some won't have to understand, they will love you and include your evolving beliefs, they trust you and have faith in your journey.

These are "your peeps", and this is the environment for your expression to flourish.

Achieve clarity about your life, have your dreams and take action, bringing them into reality.

They all live together and complement each other.

This page is for you to open your peanut

Your thoughts

Your feelings

Next steps

Υouthfulness

has very little to do with age.

Be youthful any time, let your wonder at life's richness be present.

Play fully at this game of life.

Give it your all, and don't forget - have FUN!

This page is for you to open your peanut

Your thoughts

Your feelings

Next steps

be a *Zealot*

on behalf of life!

Enthusiastically embracing your expression within all the areas of life that are important to you.

Bring zeal to your causes and make the difference.

You have the choice and the chance to contribute your light and love.

You truly are full of Wonder – Enjoy being Wonderful!

This page is for you to open your peanut

Your thoughts

Your feelings

Next steps

About the author

Avril Ann Lochhead is an enthusiastic and visionary trainer, whose results in personal empowerment are an unqualified success.

As a transitional specialist, Avril believes we can go beyond our previous thinking to access new levels of fulfilment we desire for ourselves, our families and our communities.

Embracing current circumstances, trusting an internal feeling of respect and esteem for your "Self", are the fundamental ingredients of being fulfilled.

When this relationship with yourself is regained and fully expressed, you can then expand - and offer your contribution, generosity and appreciation to others.

Your life takes on a truly magnificent flavour.

May all your peanuts be positive!

Printed in the United States
By Bookmasters